Come On In, Young Man!

Hal Lansky and Julie Lansky

With George Karalias and Keelan Parham

The story of how a young man changed
the world of fashion with the help of Bernard Lansky.

This book is dedicated to the love and memory of Bernard J. Lansky (1927-2012) who cultivated a legacy that has continued into a third generation as a lasting testament to his grandchildren, Lia, Julie, Missy, Rachel, and Rebecca, as well as his great grandchildren, Ethan, Max, Dahlia, Brianna, and Harper. His continuing kindness was a major contribution to the success of a young man who would later become a fashion icon because of Bernard's style influence. Bernard never met a stranger, and his philosophy was timeless: "You meet the same people going up the ladder as you do going down the ladder, so be nice to everyone you encounter."

Story told and inspired by Hal Lansky and Julie Lansky.
Designed and written by George Karalias
Illustrations by Keelan Parham

Published by Karalias Productions
Merrimac, Massachusetts
www.karaliasproductions.com

Lansky Brothers, Inc.
Memphis, Tennessee
www.lanskybros.com

Printed in the United States of America

First edition 2017

International Standard Book Number (ISBN) 978-0-9988057-0-2

Follow that dream, I gotta follow that dream
Keep a-movin, move along, keep a moving
I've got to follow that dream wherever that dream may lead
I've got to follow that dream to find the love I need.

- Toby Kwimper, 1962

There once was a polite and ambitious young man. He loved to look at all the colorful displays of clothes in the store windows along famous Beale Street in Memphis, Tennessee.

Mr. Lansky was standing at the door of his clothing shop, Lansky Brothers, when the young man stopped to look in his store windows.

"Come on in, young man!" he said. "It doesn't cost you anything to look around."

The young man looked up. "Thank you, Mr. Lansky! When I save up enough money, I'm gonna come in here and buy you out."

"Young man, do me a favor, don't buy me out. Just buy from me!" replied Mr. Lansky.

So in they went. With that one gesture of kindness, a friendship began. The young man's confidence started to grow.

Later, that same young man came back to see his friend, Mr. Lansky. He was looking for a new outfit. He could have gone anywhere in the big city of Memphis, but he chose to go see the man who had always been nice to him. "I need a tux for my prom, Mr. Lansky!" he said. "It's going to be at the Peabody Hotel. You know the place. It's got the ducks swimming around in the lobby!"

"Sure, I'll make you clean as 'Ajax'!" replied Mr. Lansky. "I've got just the thing for you, young man. All it needs is a hem and a home!"

And with that, the young man's pride grew. He was going to look his best when he stepped out with his girl at the prom.

During his younger years, this young man always dressed to look his best. Unlike other boys his age, he liked dress pants instead of jeans. He liked colorful shirts and jackets instead of T-shirts with rolled-up sleeves.

His friend, Mr. Lansky, was always there to advise him on how to dress.

"Fix your hair!"

"Iron your shirt!"

"Press your pants!"

"Shine your shoes!"

Mr Lansky's words rang in his ears:
"You have only one chance to make
a good first impression."

On one bright and sunny Memphis day, the young man rushed into the Lansky Brothers store on Beale Street and said, "I'm gonna be on TV, Mr. Lansky! I need you to design me a wardrobe that no one will forget!"

Mr. Lansky started pulling clothes off the racks and out of the back rooms, looking for the perfect outfit for the young man to wear on television.

As Mr. Lansky laid out all the colorful and exciting outfits, the young man timidly looked at his friend and said, "But I've got a problem, Mr. Lansky. I don't have any money."

"That is a problem, young man," he agreed, nodding his head. "Tell you what, pay me when you can. I believe in you."

Mr. Lansky gave the young man the credit and the suits he needed to help him show the world his talent and his style! Because of Mr. Lansky's support, the young man's confidence grew with each performance.

On the nights of the television shows,
Mr. Lansky watched a confident young man
who had the audience in the palm of his
hand. Local fans in and around Memphis
loved the young man so much that
in no time, national shows were
asking him to appear.

"Go, cat, go! That young man is shaking his hips and curling his lips! This seals the deal for him and his future!" thought Mr. Lansky.

Mr. Lansky was watching his friend start his journey. This young man was going places! He had a chance to become the best entertainer in the world!

Be confident and have the courage to believe in yourself! Eventually, everyone will turn to look at you. And they did. The young man was on more and more shows as he became famous.

"I wanted to say to everyone here in the studio audience, and the country, that this is a real decent, fine young man," announced Ed Sullivan, the most popular television show host of that time.

Looking at the exciting scene on the television, Mr. Lansky said, "Young man, the mirror's looking at you, and the streets want you!" The audience was going crazy over the young man's performance.

The young man never forgot the kindness Mr. Lansky showed him when he was starting out. His first big performance wouldn't have been the same if it hadn't been for Mr. Lansky's amazing outfits!

Mr. Lansky would say: "It's nice to be nice when you know you're nice."

"You meet the same people going up the ladder as you do coming down the ladder," he would add.

After the young man's appearances on the popular television shows, he would stop by the Lansky Brothers store to shop for new outfits. While there, if other customers told him how much they loved a certain shirt or a jacket, the kind young man would insist on buying it for them. He would say, "Mr. Lansky, make sure this item goes to my friend here, and put it on my bill."

The young man was grateful to those who had seen something special in him at the very beginning of his career. Mr. Lansky was one of those people. The young man was always gracious and perfectly charming—he had the manners of a true Southern gentleman.

Some things just go
together naturally,
like confidence and
style. You can create
your own trend.
"They go together like
a stamp and a letter!"
was how Mr. Lansky
would describe it.

People were always surprised by the young man's performances. There were many who would write him letters to tell him that they loved him.

There were also those who were not too happy with his concerts and felt his dancing should be banned.

The young man would say: "I never want to upset anyone. The way I sing and dance and move are my way of expressing myself."

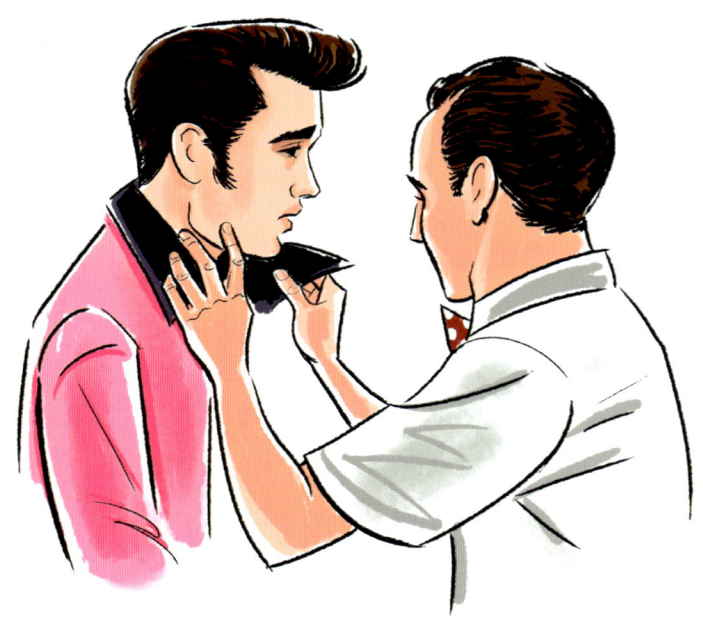

When you look good, you feel confident. When you are confident, you can do anything! As the young man became a rising star, more and more people were inspired by him and dressed like him!

They flipped their collars!

They loved the pink-and-black outfits that Mr. Lansky created for the young man!

They wore blue suede shoes for a while, and then they wore white boots matching the ones the young man liked so much!

They mixed stripes with plaids because that's what the young man did!

The matching color combinations looked great!

Some makers of clothes thought the young man was a "sloppy dresser" and one of the worst dressers in the country! But most people knew better! The young man's friend, Mr. Lansky, made sure everyone knew it too! Just because the young man had his own style, that didn't mean he was wrong or sloppy! He was confident in his style, and he set the trend for others to follow.

Young people were crazy about wearing the clothes that made them feel good! They wanted to have the same confidence that the young man showed when he was singing in front of millions of people.

Don't let go of your dreams. Stay confident!

Mr. Lansky would tell his friends in Memphis, "Don't let anyone fool you, this kid's a sharp dresser! Some of his outfits are out of this world! He's breaking all the rules. He's recording in his own style and he's dressing in his own style."

He would tell the young man,

"Like a broken drum, you can't be beat!"

In Hollywood, the young man started his career as an actor. He starred in more than thirty movies. He was showing off even more popular styles and new ways of dressing to impress.

The young man was so popular that he couldn't visit Mr. Lansky's store during the day any more. If he did, so many people would try to catch a glimpse of him or get his autograph that all the daily activity on famous Beale Street would come to a complete stop!

"We'll open our store at midnight, and you can come pick out what you want!" announced Mr. Lansky.

Early on, Mr. Lansky, and in later years, his son, Hal, would load up the Lansky truck with new clothes and make a personal delivery to the young man's home. The truck would always return to the store empty!

Mr. Lansky would say, "You pop the whip, and we'll make the trip! Don't stop now, you're on a roll!" as the young man was picking out his favorite outfits.

Wherever the young man went, everyone would ask him where he got his great-looking clothes! "From Lansky's on Beale Street in Memphis!" he would say to them.

The young man was always grateful to Mr. Lansky and made sure all his close musician friends in Memphis went to visit Mr. Lansky—Johnny Cash, Carl Perkins, Jerry Lee Lewis, Sam Phillips of Sun Records, and so many more.

They all stopped by to see Mr. Lansky for the latest look!

Over time, the young man and his three friends, Johnny, Carl, and Jerry Lee became known as the "Million Dollar Quartet."

Just like the music that all the artists wrote and sang, originality was the trademark of Lansky's style.

A good style comes with a good feeling, and looking good never goes out of style!

"I like this look, Mr. Lansky" said the young man.
"You're number one! You deserve it," replied Mr. Lansky.

If you haven't guessed already, this young man, whom
Mr. Lansky encouraged and styled in the finest outfits, was
The King of Rock 'n' Roll, Elvis Presley,
the greatest entertainer the world has ever known.

We can all follow our dreams.
This is your chance.

Dress the part and look your best.
The whole world is watching.

Believe in yourself, and everyone will believe in you.

Have confidence in yourself, and have confidence in those around you.

They'll always remember you for it.

"Thank you, Mr. Lansky.
Thank you very much ...
for everything"

"Please ... call me Bernard."

"Yes sir, Mr. Lansky."

"Remember, the mirror's looking at you,
and the streets want you, Elvis."

In Loving Memory of both these wonderful men who shaped a generation.

As Bernard Lansky always said: "May we always have the style of Elvis!"

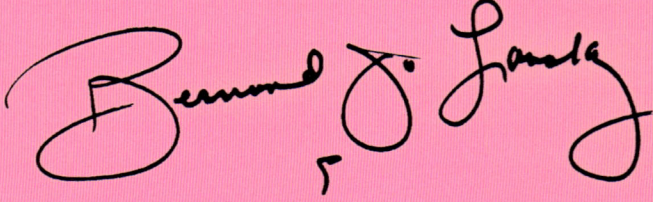